CRL

SOUTH AMERICA

ATLANTIC OCEAN

BOLIVIA

PARAGUAY

CHILE

ARGENTINA

URUGUAY

PACIFIC OCEAN

Congratulations! You've been selected to take part in a 12-day exploration of the Amazonian rainforest in Brazil where you'll have a chance to see and study hundreds of fascinating jungle animals.

In particular, we would like you to try to spot a rare harpy eagle and report back to the research centre on the sighting and location.

Please check the enclosed tickets and itinerary carefully and study the suggested packing list. A pack of background information is included to get you started. You will be required to attend and pass a medical before you travel. Details are enclosed. The necessary injections for typhoid, hepatitis A and yellow fever and a tetanus booster (if required) will be given to you at that medical along with a supply of antimalarial tablets for the trip.

We look forward to welcoming you at Manaus on 1 June. Good luck!

Yours sincerely,

Russell Stevenson (Research Officer)

Jane Dix (Research Officer)

Harpy eagle

The harpy eagle is the world's largest eagle. It grows up to 90 cm tall and has a wingspan of nearly 2 m. Its huge feet end in long, sharp talons, each as big as a human adult male's hand, with which it grabs its prey from treetop branches. Harpy eagles are found in rainforests from South Mexico to North Argentina. They eat sloths, porcupines, curassows, macaws and monkeys. The harpy's nest is a platform of sticks, built in tall rainforest trees around 45 m above the forest floor. The bird is believed to lay two eggs at a time and the young stay with their parents for up to a year. Harpy eagles are now rare, mainly due to the destruction of their habitat and hunting by man.

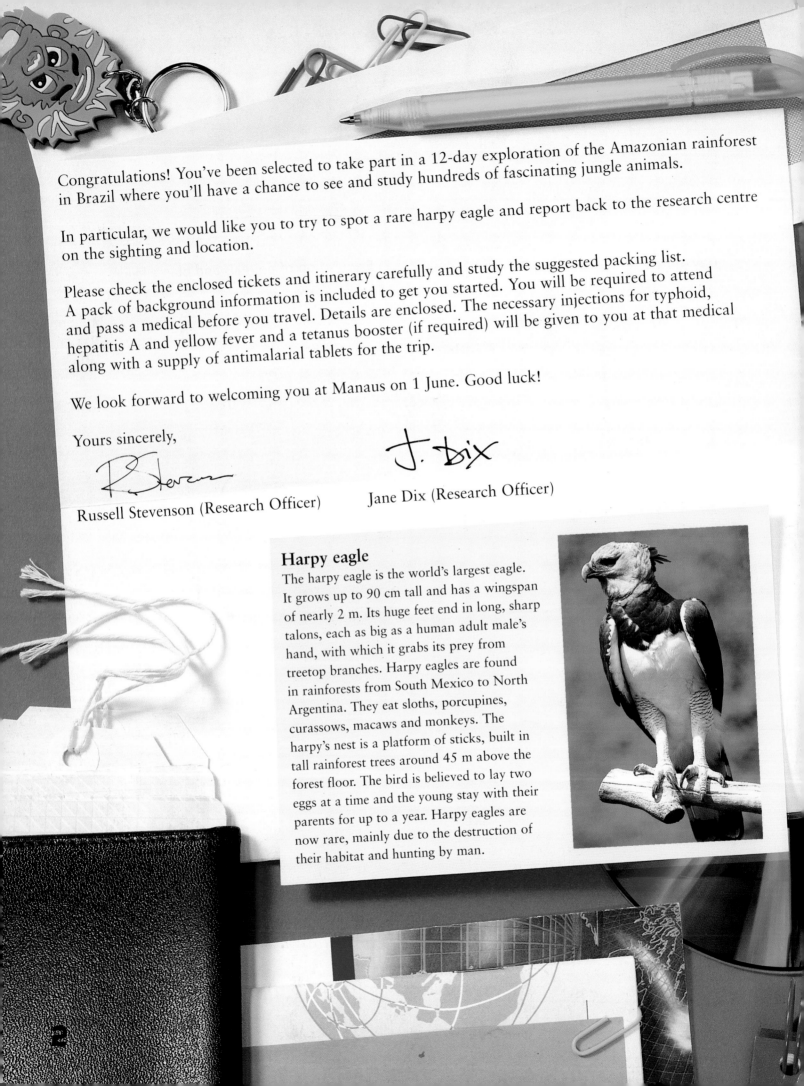

Itinerary

Day 1: Arrival and orientation
Meet research team at Manaus airport; welcome dinner at hotel
• The world's rainforests • Rainforest animals
• Rainforest trees • Climate • Amazon tribes

Days 2–4: The river
Three-day trip up the river by boat then canoe to base camp, studying river life and river water
• River water • Jaguars, tapirs and capybara
• Amazon fish • Endangered river animals

Day 5: The forest floor
Exploration of animals and plants living on the forest floor
• Butterflies and moths • Camouflage
• Mimicry • Ants • Living in groups
• Rainforest soil • Plant defences

Day 6: The understorey
Exploration of animals and plants living in the understorey
• Lianas, climbers and stranglers • Epiphytes
• Drip tips • Snakes • Tree frogs • Sloths

Day 7: The canopy
Exploration of animals and plants living in the canopy
• Climbing into the canopy • Study of a treetop bromeliad • Treetop lifecycles • Canopy birds
• Bats • Monkeys

Night 9: The rainforest at night
Creatures of the night
• Nocturnal animals • Night monkey
• Night-time predators • Bats

Days 9–12: Departure
• Ecotourism • Conserving the rainforest
• Medicine

Clearing the rainforest

Environmental report

The world's rainforests are being cut down for timber such as teak and mahogany, for mining, for cattle ranching and for plantations. Because of the huge diversity of life in just a small part of a rainforest, some scientists estimate that ten species of plants and animals are becoming extinct every day as the rainforests are cleared. Scientists also fear that the destruction of the rainforests is changing the world's climate. Like other green plants, rainforests take in carbon dioxide gas from the atmosphere when they make food and give out oxygen, which animals need to breathe. When rainforests are cleared and burned, there are fewer plants to absorb the carbon dioxide and a lot of carbon is released, making the Earth's climate hotter and contributing to the greenhouse effect. Poverty has forced people into the forests, where they scratch a living chopping down trees and planting crops in cleared ground. Crops cannot be grown for long in the poor rainforest soil, so people have to move on to "slash and burn" a new area of forest.

Huge areas of the Brazilian rainforest have been cleared to enlarge cattle ranches.

Suggested packing list

Equipment:
- Binoculars
- Camera
- Specimen jars
- Torch
- Hammock*
- Mosquito net*
- Sealed bags filled with silica ←
- Sunglasses
- Watercolours
- Pens and coloured pencils
- Notebook
- Sketchpad
- Clipboard
- Reference book on rainforest plants and animals

Get camera that takes instant photos!

To stop equipment growing fungus and mould on it in hot, wet rainforest!!!

Suggested medical kit:
- Sunscreen lotion
- Insect repellent
- Water-purification tablets
- Aspirin or paracetamol, for fever
- Antihistamine (in case of insect bites or to prevent motion sickness)
- Kaolin and pectin preparation for stomach upsets
- Rehydration mixture for severe diarrhoea
- Antiseptic cream and antibiotic powder for minor injuries
- Calamine lotion for insect bites and stings
- Bandages and bandaids
- Scissors, tweezers and thermometer

Take personal stereo and tapes!

Get more camera film!

Clothing:
- Boots
- Underpants (5 pairs) and cotton socks (5 pairs)
- Long trousers (3 pairs)
- Long-sleeved shirts (3)
- Hat

* Please note: Hammocks and mosquito nets are provided
at the base camp but many explorers prefer to bring their own.

Information for explorers: Malaria

Malaria is a serious disease transmitted to humans by the malaria-transmitting *Anopheles* mosquitoes. Symptoms of malaria include headaches, fever, chills and sweating. To avoid, take the recommended antimalarial drugs which kill parasites in their first stage of development.

Malaria prevention

Mosquitoes, including *Anopheles*, like to feed at night, from dusk until dawn. Explorers should:

- wear light-coloured clothing
- wear long pants and long-sleeved shirts
- use insect repellent on all exposed skin
- avoid wearing perfume or aftershave
- use a mosquito net impregnated with insect repellent
- take antimalarial drugs

Other diseases spread by mosquitoes

Dengue fever: Symptoms include fever, headaches, muscle pain, followed by a rash. Full recovery can take a month.

Yellow fever: Symptoms include fever, headache, abdominal pain and vomiting. There is no known treatment apart from trying to keep the fever low and drinking plenty of fluids. Yellow fever vaccine highly recommended (gives protection for ten years).

Mefloquine

Course to commence 2–3 weeks before travel and continue 4 weeks after return

Adult dosage: One 250 mg tablet once a week
Child (up to 12 years) dosage: Three-quarters of a tablet once a week

Have just read that you can get all sorts of other stuff like fungal infections (athlete's foot or crotch rot. Yuk!). Must also drink only purified water or water that's been boiled for at least five minutes so I don't get the runs!

Day 1: Evening

I'm here, at last! Arrived in Manaus late this afternoon and met Jane and Russell, the research scientists. We've just had a brilliant meal of grilled dourado fish, and I tried a fruit drink called guaraná made from the berry of a plant growing in the Amazon. I've been spending the last hour or so looking through the information pack Russell and Jane gave me about rainforests. Have just read that:

• rainforests are home to around half of the world's total species of plants and animals – and MILLIONS of species probably haven't even been discovered yet!

• rainforests are the most complex ecosystems in the world, with the greatest biodiversity, or variety, of plants and animal life.

The River Negro – took this from the plane before landing in Manaus

Asia's tigers at risk

Environmental report

Many of the world's rainforest animals are in danger of extinction because of the destruction of huge areas of tropical forest. Across much of Asia, vast tropical and deciduous forests have been cut down for wood or to clear land for farming. As a result, Bali and Javan tigers are extinct and other tigers, including Sumatran, Bengal and Indochinese tigers, are now endangered. Figures released by conservationists estimate that there are only 5,000–7,000 tigers remaining in the wild, down from 100,000 at the beginning of the last century.

The Bengal tiger, found mainly in India, is now an endangered species.

Tried some cupuaçu. Tasted creamy and a bit chocolatey!

8

Amazonia
Lodge Hotel

◆

FRUIT DRINKS

Guaraná
Carambola
Pupunha
Maracujá
Goiaba
Tapereba
Sorva
Mari-mari
Cupuaçu
Piranga
Inga
Abiu
Seriguela
Bacuri
Jambo

DAY 1

Rainforest animals

The hot, humid rainforests are teeming with life. Because competition for food and space is fierce, many creatures have adapted by developing special features or behaviour to help them survive. As a result, there are millions of species of plants and animals living in the world's rainforests.

The southern cassowary lives in rainforests in New Guinea and northern Australia.

The gentle, sociable **gorilla** lives in parts of the African rainforest.

The orang-utan is confined to the rainforests of Borneo and Sumatra in Indonesia. It lives alone, in pairs or in small family groups.

The slender loris inhabits the rainforests of Sri Lanka and southern India.

RAINFORESTS OF THE WORLD

CENTRAL AMERICA

SOUTH AMERICA

Equator

AFRICA

INDIA

SRI LANKA

MADAGASCAR

SOUTHEAST ASIA

NEW GUINEA

AUSTRALIA

I'm here – the AMAZON rainforest – the **biggest** rainforest in the world!

Rainforest facts

- Most rainforests grow in the tropics.
- Tropical rainforests are hot, wet and steamy, with an average temperature of over 28°C, average rainfall of 200–1,000 cm and average humidity of around 82%.
- The largest rainforests are in Brazil (South America), Zaire (Africa) and Indonesia (Southeast Asia).
- Rainforests used to cover 14% of the Earth's surface. Today they cover less than 6%, but still contain nearly 60% of the world's total species of plants and animals.
- Rainforests took around 70–100 million years to grow and evolve.

Amazonian facts

• The Amazon rainforest is 6.5 million sq km, taking up two-fifths of South America and 36% of Brazil.

• The Amazon River is 6,275 km long – making it the world's second-longest river after the Nile in Africa – and its mouth, where it meets the sea, is around 320 km wide.

• An estimated 1,100 tributaries flow into the Amazon. The whole river system carries around 20% of the world's fresh water.

• The Amazon River has more tributaries than any other river in the world.

• The vast Amazon rainforest stretches into nine different countries in South America.

Notes on the rainforest

The rainforest, or jungle, can be divided into layers:

• <u>Emergent trees</u> – really tall trees, some growing up to 55 m high, breaking through the canopy.

• <u>Canopy</u> – an almost unbroken layer of treetops, making a kind of thick, green ceiling to the forest.

• <u>Understorey</u> – smaller and younger trees (saplings), shrubs and tangled vines under the canopy.

• <u>Forest floor</u> – almost bare and quite dark, with a thin layer of rotting vegetation over poor, tropical soil.

Most rainforest animals, such as birds, monkeys and tree frogs, live in the canopy.

Can't wait to see some of them!
(It would be great if I saw a harpy eagle so that I can report back to the research centre!)

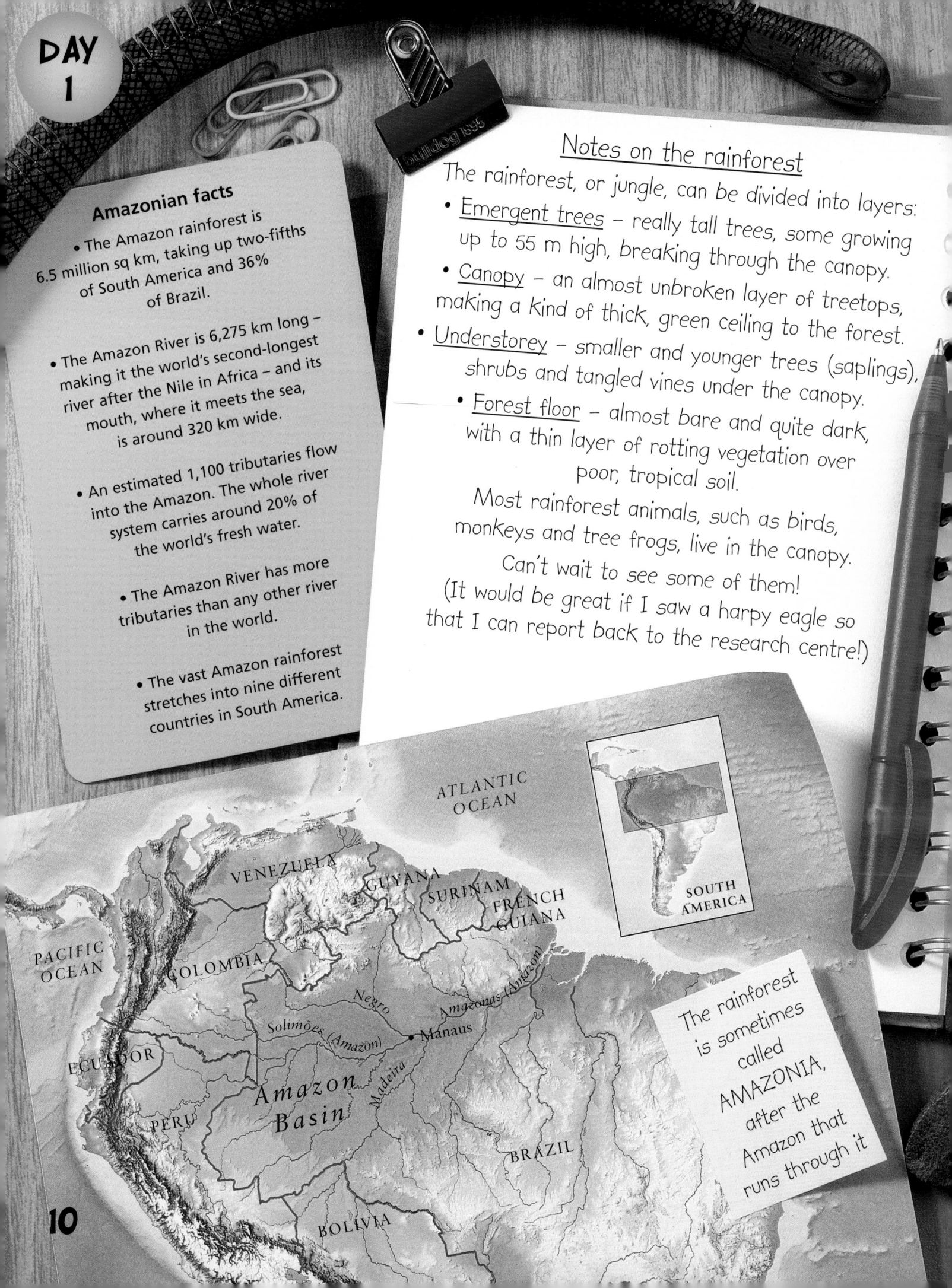

ATLANTIC OCEAN

VENEZUELA

GUYANA

SURINAM

FRENCH GUIANA

SOUTH AMERICA

PACIFIC OCEAN

COLOMBIA

Negro

Amazonas (Amazon)

Solimões (Amazon)

Manaus

ECUADOR

Amazon Basin

Madeira

PERU

BRAZIL

BOLIVIA

The rainforest is sometimes called AMAZONIA, after the Amazon that runs through it

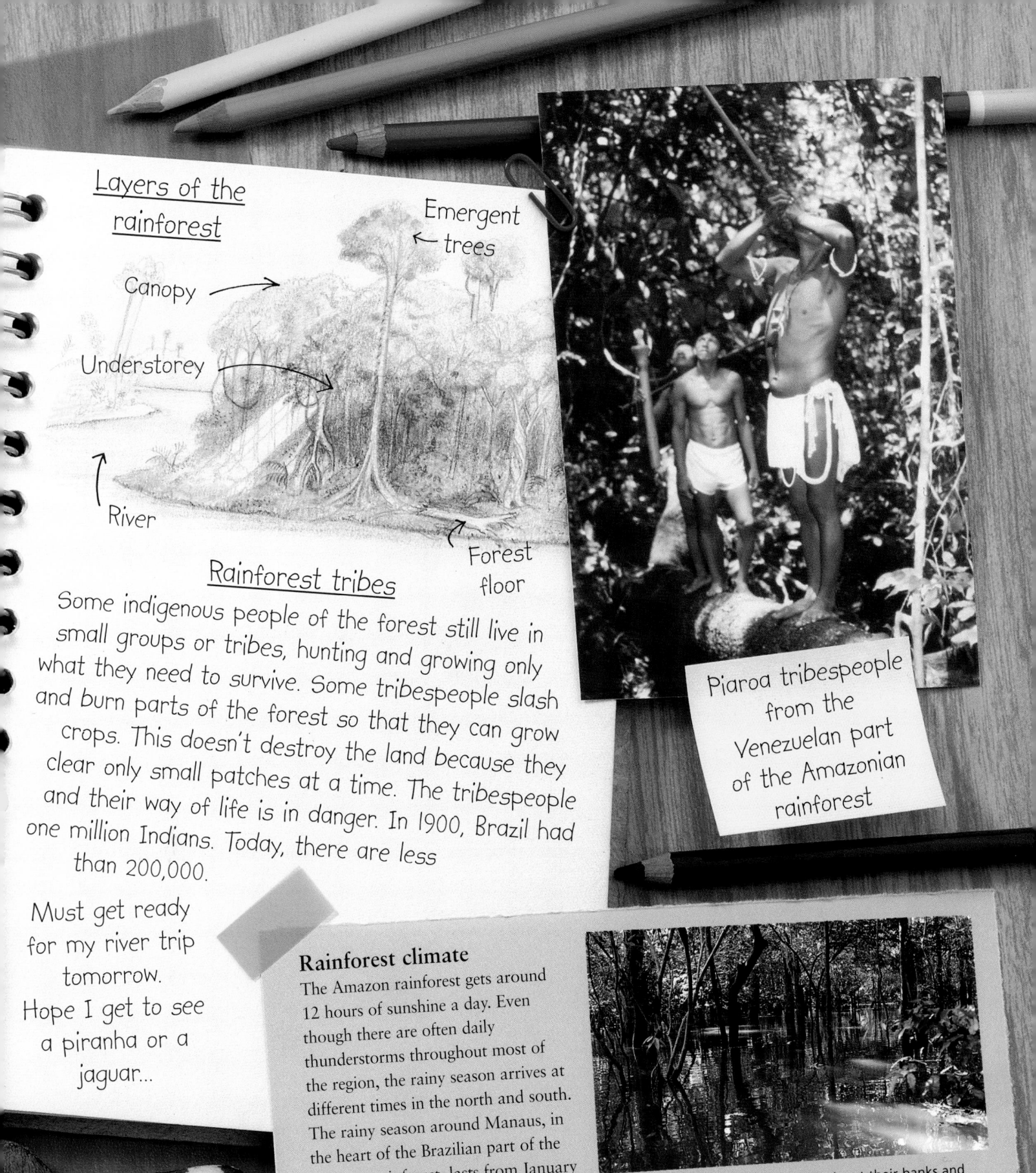

Layers of the rainforest

Emergent trees

Canopy

Understorey

River

Forest floor

Rainforest tribes

Some indigenous people of the forest still live in small groups or tribes, hunting and growing only what they need to survive. Some tribespeople slash and burn parts of the forest so that they can grow crops. This doesn't destroy the land because they clear only small patches at a time. The tribespeople and their way of life is in danger. In 1900, Brazil had one million Indians. Today, there are less than 200,000.

Must get ready for my river trip tomorrow.
Hope I get to see a piranha or a jaguar...

Piaroa tribespeople from the Venezuelan part of the Amazonian rainforest

Rainforest climate

The Amazon rainforest gets around 12 hours of sunshine a day. Even though there are often daily thunderstorms throughout most of the region, the rainy season arrives at different times in the north and south. The rainy season around Manaus, in the heart of the Brazilian part of the Amazon rainforest, lasts from January to June, with temperatures of around 35°C and a relative humidity of up to 98 %. The average yearly rainfall is high, at 2,000 mm.

During the rainy season, many rivers burst their banks and parts of the forest become flooded, sometimes up to a depth of 10 m and 10 km into the forest. The flooded forest may stretch around 100,000 sq kms (or 2% of the total region of the rainforest).

Day 4: The river

We've been travelling up the river for nearly three days now. The wide part of the Amazon we came up first was quite muddy and dark so I didn't see any fish. We did spot quite a few animals by the banks, though, including some spectacled caiman. We switched to a much smaller boat yesterday and we've been chugging up a narrower tributary.

Saw these MASSIVE water lilies yesterday – the flowers are bigger than my head!

Giant water lilies

Piranha fish

Razor-sharp triangular teeth and strong jaws!

I've been collecting different samples of river water. One small stream was so clear I could see right down to the tangled roots at the bottom and GUESS WHAT, I saw a shoal of red-bellied fish which were piranha! WHOA!

Also saw this anaconda near the far bank.

Anaconda slithering onto the river bank – must have been around 8 m long!

14

Whitewater - looks like milky coffee

River water experiment

Clearwater - looks like weak green tea

Studying river water samples for colour and transparency then testing their pH values (to see how acidic they are):

1. "Whitewater" – brownish, muddy-looking, hard to see through – pH value of 7 (neutral)

2. "Clearwater" – greenish colour, transparent – pH value about halfway between whitewater and blackwater

3. "Blackwater" – dark brown or reddish, transparent – pH value of about 4

Blackwater is the most acidic water. Russell says it has fewer minerals and nutrients than whitewater.

Blackwater - so dark it looks like flat cola!

River waters

The main Amazon river is called "whitewater" but is really a browny colour. It is rich in nutrients from sediment carried down from the Andes Mountains. "Clearwater" and "blackwater" are much poorer in nutrients. Most plants and animals live in or along whitewater rivers. There are often great numbers of fish in blackwater streams, but they depend mainly on insects, fruit or pollen falling into the water from the surrounding forest rather than nutrients in the water itself.

Meeting of the blackwater Rio Negro and the whitewater River Solimões near Manaus.

Rainforest swimmers

Most rainforest animals are good swimmers. They need to be because there is as much water as land in the Amazon Basin, especially during the rainy season when many rivers burst their banks.

Even though cats usually hate the water, jaguars swim well and sometimes feed on fish. They also hunt capybaras (rodents), peccaries (small pigs) and tapirs.

The capybara is a good swimmer and diver and spends a lot of its time in the rivers and streams. Its eyes, ears and nostrils are high on its head so they stay clear of the water and its feet are partly webbed so they can act as tiny paddles to help it swim.

The tapir swims in rivers to wash, escape from predators and to find food

Pirarucu

Range: Tropical South America
Habitat: Rivers, swamps
Size: Up to 4 m
Features: Probably the largest freshwater fish in the world, weighing up to 200 kg. Has a large swim bladder which can be used as a lung.

Amazon fish

Scientists estimate that there are over 1,500 species of fish in the Amazon River system, and probably many more still undiscovered. The huge variety of fish reflects the diversity of Amazon water, which is fast-flowing and clear in some places and slow and muddy in others. As a result, fish of various families (such as the characin family which includes the neon tetra and piranha) have a wide range of colours and habits.

The 1 metre-long aruana fish feeds on fish, insects and spiders. It can also jump out of the water to grab a bird or even a baby sloth from overhanging branches or the trunk of a tree.

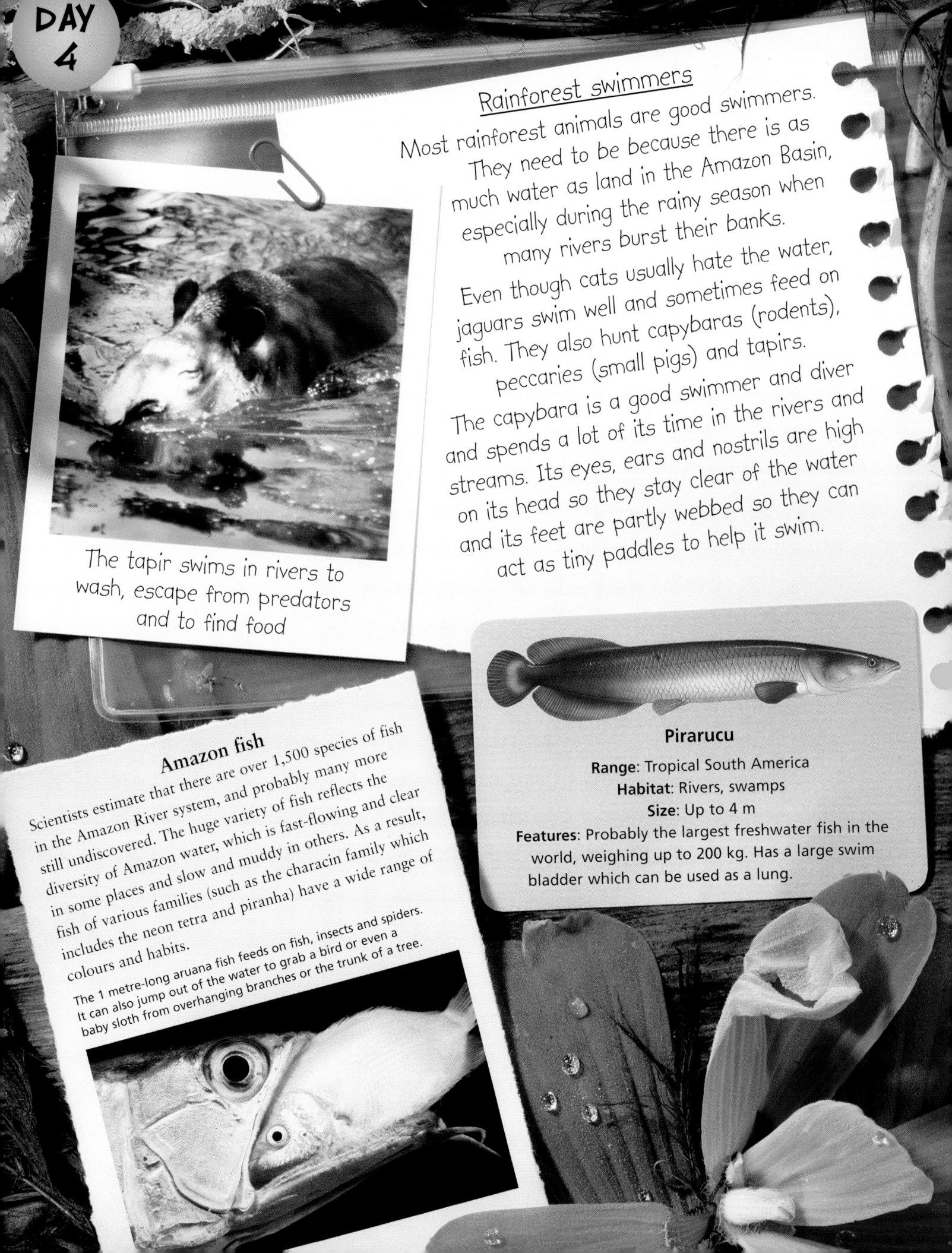

River animals under threat

Environmental report

Despite being protected by law, hunting continues of the spectacled caiman and its much rarer relative, the black caiman, both for food and their skins. The young are also collected and sold as pets, or even stuffed and sold as curios. The black caiman is the longest animal in Amazon waters, with adults

Spectacled caiman by the Amazon

Capybara with babies

reaching 5 or 6 m. The smaller spectacled caiman grows around 2.5 m long. However, because of hunting, adults of both species rarely reach full-grown sizes.

Another animal hunted intensively for food throughout most of the Amazon is the capybara. Some capybara populations have even left the river banks where they usually live during the day to hide in the forest, only emerging at night to feed.

If in danger, hoatzin chicks jump out of the nest and dive into the river below to escape

Hoatzin bird in its nest over a riverbank – a clumsy flier but its chicks can swim!

Candiru

Range: South America: Amazon Basin
Habitat: Rivers, streams
Size: 2.5 cm
Features: Parasitic; feeds on the blood of other fishes. May also enter the body of humans or other mammals through the urethra, as they bathe or pass water (it swims up the stream of urine); extremely difficult and painful to remove.

Yuk!! Don't think I'll go swimming then!

Neon tetra

Range: Northern South America, Amazon Basin
Habitat: Rivers, streams
Size: 4 cm
Features: Feeds mainly on seeds and fruit that have fallen into streams from trees. Its bigger relative, the piranha, feeds mainly on fish, fruit and seeds but will also attack larger, usually wounded, animals.

Type of water lettuce that floats on the Amazon River

Day 5: The forest floor

We finally reached base camp late last night. I was glad to fall into my hammock. It was strange, though, sleeping under a mosquito net. I spent most of today exploring the forest floor in a clearing near camp. Saw some beautiful blue morpho butterflies, zillions of tiny leaf-cutter ants marching in rows up and down branches and tree-trunks, and beetles, centipedes and millipedes part-hidden in the soil.

Startled a coral pipesnake which slithered into its burrow, leaving just its tail poking out. This snake is sometimes called a false coral snake because its bright colours and markings are similar to those of a poisonous cousin.

Jane helped me entice a nocturnal tarantula out of its hole with a twig!

← HERE IT IS!

Coral pipesnake – looks poisonous but it's not!

Tarantula – around 15 cm wide with legs outstretched!

Owl butterfly caterpillars munching on a leaf

Butterfly or moth? (main differences)

Underside of wings →

88 butterfly (wingspan 4 cm)

- Clubbed antennae
- Rests with wings folded back
- Flies during the day
- Thin body (not hairy)

- Straight antennae
- Fat, furry body
- Rests with wings stretched out

Giant agrippa moth
(wingspan 25 cm)

- Most moths fly at night (I saw this one camouflaged on tree-trunk)

Warning signs

Some butterflies of the same species fly together in large groups so that predators can easily recognise their bold colours and markings, which warn that they do not taste good to eat. Other butterflies (such as the postman butterfly) mimic these warning colours and the mimicry is often enough for a predator to avoid them.

Postman butterfly with "warning" colours and markings.

Blue morpho
Range: Central and South America
Habitat: Rainforest
Wingspan: 8–14 cm
Features: Shimmering deep metallic blue wings; feeds on juices of fallen fruit.

Queen Alexandra's birdwing
Range: Papua New Guinea
Habitat: Rainforest
Wingspan: Up to 30 cm
Features: Female is the largest butterfly in the world. Species is now rare and protected. Both male and female are poisonous.

Katydid beetle disguised as a leaf!

Found this dead longhorn beetle on the way back to camp. It would soon have been eaten up in hours by all kinds of creatures living on the forest floor so I was lucky to get it in one piece!

Hide and seek

Small creatures have many ways of hiding from predators. Some hide under a leaf or in the bark of a tree. Others use camouflage. A moth's speckled brown wings help it hide against a tree-trunk and the speckled, blotched skin of a lizard blends in with the dark forest floor.

An army of leafcutter ants carries torn leaves back to their nest, which they tend in fungus gardens. Their larvae feed on fungus growing on the leaves.

Social living

Some insects, such as ants, termites and some bees and wasps, live in colonies. There is security in living in a large group. If large numbers are eaten or destroyed, there are plenty more to carry on so the colony survives. One of the main predators of ants and termites is the anteater, which breaks open nests or mounds with its strong front claws and slurps up insects, larvae and eggs on its long, sticky tongue.

Giant male Hercules beetles fighting

Beetles have armour to protect themselves from predators, such as birds, lizards and small mammals. Their hard front wing cases cover their delicate back wings

Looking at soil and leaf litter

There's no thick, rotting pile of leaf litter on the rainforest floor like you often get in temperate, deciduous forests. Any leaves, twigs, branches or fallen fruit and flowers decompose (rot) quickly because it's so hot and humid. They're also broken down by termites, worms, fungi and microscopic organisms, such as bacteria, in the soil. There are millions of these decomposers and they work so quickly, most of the soil is thin and poor in nutrients. Any goodness is found in the top, shallow layer of humus, or decomposed organic matter.

Huge buttress roots grow above the ground, helping to support tall trees

<u>Temperate woodland tree</u> (where most of nutrients are in the soil). Longer roots dig down into richer soil to take in minerals and water.

<u>Rainforest tree</u> (where most nutrients are in the living plants and trees themselves).

Lots of shallow roots in top layer of soil where most water and minerals are found.

Plants fight back

Environmental report

Rainforest plants and trees are constantly under attack, night and day, from millions of creatures that feed on their leaves or hollow out their trunks to make nests. As a result, plants have all kinds of ways of defending themselves. Some have developed toxins to poison would-be leaf-eaters. Others are covered with spikes and thorns to make them difficult to eat. One plant is even home to a colony of ants that charges out to see off any other insect that tries to eat its leaves.

Picked up these spiny leaves. They're from the Ananas (pineapple) family. Would be tough to eat!

It seems to rain hard here at least once a day, but not for long.
Temperature: 28.5°C
Humidity: 96% (partly caused by <u>transpiration</u> – the process in which plants give off water when they make food.)

Day 6: The understorey

Spent the morning studying the understorey. It's really <u>dark</u> because not much sunlight gets through the thick layer of green canopy leaves above.

• Tree with roots like <u>stilts</u> to hold it up in the thin soil and help it grow towards the sunlight. Roots grow down to the ground from trunk or branches.

• Roots of a <u>strangler fig</u> wrapped round and round a tree.

dangling ← aerial roots

• Plants (called <u>epiphytes</u>), growing high up on tree trunks and branches.

• Climbing plants and woody vines loop round tree trunks like spaghetti. Their <u>tendrils</u> wrap themselves around other plants ← for support.

Passionflower

curling stem

Passionflowers grow from the shady forest floor up through the canopy towards the light

Large, ripe jackfruits growing on a tree. These fruits are cultivated in clearings in the rainforest

Looking at leaves

Some low-growing leaves are thin and wide to catch as much sunlight as possible so that they can make food through photosynthesis.

Other leaves have a thick, waxy surface to help stop insects and other animals eating them and mosses from growing on them. A lot of leaves are long with pointed ends called drip tips. Rain runs off the leaves so that pools of water don't collect on them.

How a drip tip works

Water droplets

Pointed end →

This helps to keep the leaves dry, otherwise they'd soon be covered in lichens, algae and mosses.

Understorey plants

Many understorey plants have adapted so that they can grow in low sunlight. Not many flowers and fruits grow in this part of the rainforest. If they do, they are usually large and pale to stand out so that animals will feed on them and help to pollinate them or spread their seeds. Epiphytes grow on other plants. They have roots that either fix themselves to the supporting plant or roots that are long and hang down to take in water and nutrients from the air. Stranglers start out as epiphytes. Their seeds are dropped by a bird or bat onto a treetop branch. Long roots grow down the tree to the ground. Eventually, the strangler's roots cover the tree and it rots and dies.

A web of twisting lianas climb around most rainforest trees.

• Glossy, waxy surface so water runs off

← Water drips off here

Day 6: Evening

I can hear all Kinds of bird calls and crashing sounds through the branches above my head, but it's hard to spot any animals because they're so well camouflaged. Hope something comes out of the trees!

Barred leaf frog camouflaged against a leaf

Common iguana

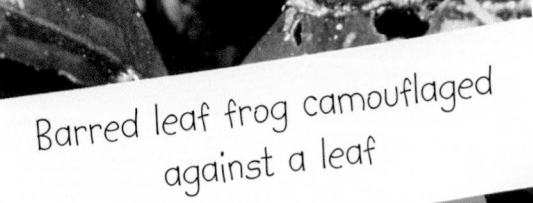

Long toes and nails

Life in the understorey

Many animals that live in the understorey are small and lightweight with sharp claws to help them grip tightly to trees and vines, and long tails which they use for balance and to wrap around branches so they don't fall. They often come down to the forest floor to feed. Some can move fairly quickly, scuttling along branches to hide in the hollow of a tree or among leaves. If scared, the iguana can drop 20–30 m to the ground or into water to escape from danger. The emerald tree boa, one of the fastest-moving boa snakes, strikes quickly, squeezing its prey to death in its coils.

Long tail

↑ Managed to get this photo of a frog though – it uses sticky pads on its toes to cling to a slippery stem or leaf.

Keeping in touch

Nocturnal curassow

Some animals rely on loud calls to communicate with others in the deep shade of the understorey. The toró spiny rat's loud *tow-row!* call can be heard day and night. Curassow males sing only at night, although they search for food during the day. Their booming calls are used in courtship and to threaten other males.

Hiding out

Many understorey animals are camouflaged to hide from predators or lie in wait to surprise their prey. The white flecks along the back of an emerald tree boa break up dappled sunlight. The iguana can camouflage itself against leaves or bark by changing the colour of its skin to different shades of green and brown.

Arrow-poison frog with blotched yellow and black skin.

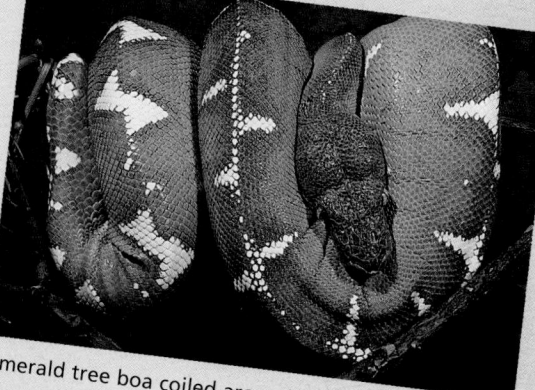

Emerald tree boa coiled around a branch.

Being bold

Other animals are brightly coloured to warn predators that they are dangerous. One species, the golden arrow-poison frog, has enough venom in its skin to kill over 2,000 people. The poison is extracted by local tribespeople and used on the tips of arrows for hunting.

Three-toed sloth S L O W L Y climbing down a tree

The so-slow sloth...

Here are some sloth facts I've been finding out:

- Because it spends most of its life hanging upside-down, its fur is parted along its stomach (not down its back like other animals) so that rainwater can run off.

- Algae living in its fur make it look a greenish colour.

- Its claws are so strong, it can remain hanging upside-down for three days or so even when it is dead.

- It climbs slowly, moving one limb at a time.

- It grows to about 75 cm long.

- It can only drag its body on the ground, but is a good swimmer.

Canopy facts

• The canopy is formed by crowns of trees around 30 to 40 m high, with taller emergent trees breaking through.

• Most rainforest animals live in the canopy and many never descend to the ground.

• Most canopy animals are herbivores, eating leaves, fruit, seeds and nuts.

• Many vines and climbers that grow through the understorey flower in the canopy layer, in the sun.

• Most canopy leaves have drip tips so that water runs off their surface.

There's just been another hard shower of rain – you should hear the frogs croaking. It's deafening!

It's hotter up here in the canopy but not as humid as it was yesterday, down in the understorey!
Temperature: 31.5°C
Humidity: 60%

Day 7: The canopy

Hard to believe, but I'm sitting on a tiny wooden platform in the canopy, about 40 m above the ground. It was scary climbing up because you have to sit in a harness, put your feet in stirrups and then use a kind of pulley to hoist yourself up, one leg at a time.

Russell hauling himself up the tree

Our wooden platform, high in the canopy

Wooden walkway between platforms

Flock of scarlet macaws flying past our platform!

Looking at life in a treetop bromeliad

"My" bromeliad (<u>Neoregelia carolinae</u>)

Pool of water (must hold around 50 litres of water!)

Damsel fly

Tree frog

Crab

Worm

Watertight cup of leaves

Mosquito larvae

Have just read that the mosquitoes that carry malaria (and yellow fever) mostly live in the canopy, where they feed on the blood of monkeys and other animals. Only the females bite, mostly at dawn and dusk.

Bromeliads – miniature rainforest gardens

Bromeliads are epiphytes and members of the pineapple family that grow on the branches of trees. Their thick, waxy leaves are arranged in a cup that catches and stores rainwater and debris, such as leaves, falling from taller trees in the canopy. The water and decomposing litter provide nutrients for the plants themselves and for animals living in them. Some bromeliads can hold up to 55 litres of water and may be home to worms, snakes, frogs, insects, spiders and even small mammals.

Rainwater runs down a bromeliad's curved spiky leaves into a watertight tank in the centre of the plant.

Treetop lifecycles

Bromeliads play an important role in the lifecycle of some rainforest animals. For example, the female strawberry arrow-poison frog (right), which lives in the tropical forests of Central America, carries her newly hatched tadpoles to a pool of water in the base of a bromeliad. There, the tadpoles develop and grow into adults, feeding on infertile eggs brought by the mother.

Many insects, such as mosquitoes, lay their eggs in water in bromeliads. The trapped water provides the perfect feeding and growing environment for the aquatic larvae that hatch from the eggs. The larvae become pupae and, a few days later, an adult mosquito emerges from each pupal case.

1. Eggs laid on leaf.

2. Tadpoles hatch and wriggle onto mother's back.

3. Mother carries tadpoles to treetop bromeliad where they grow into frogs.

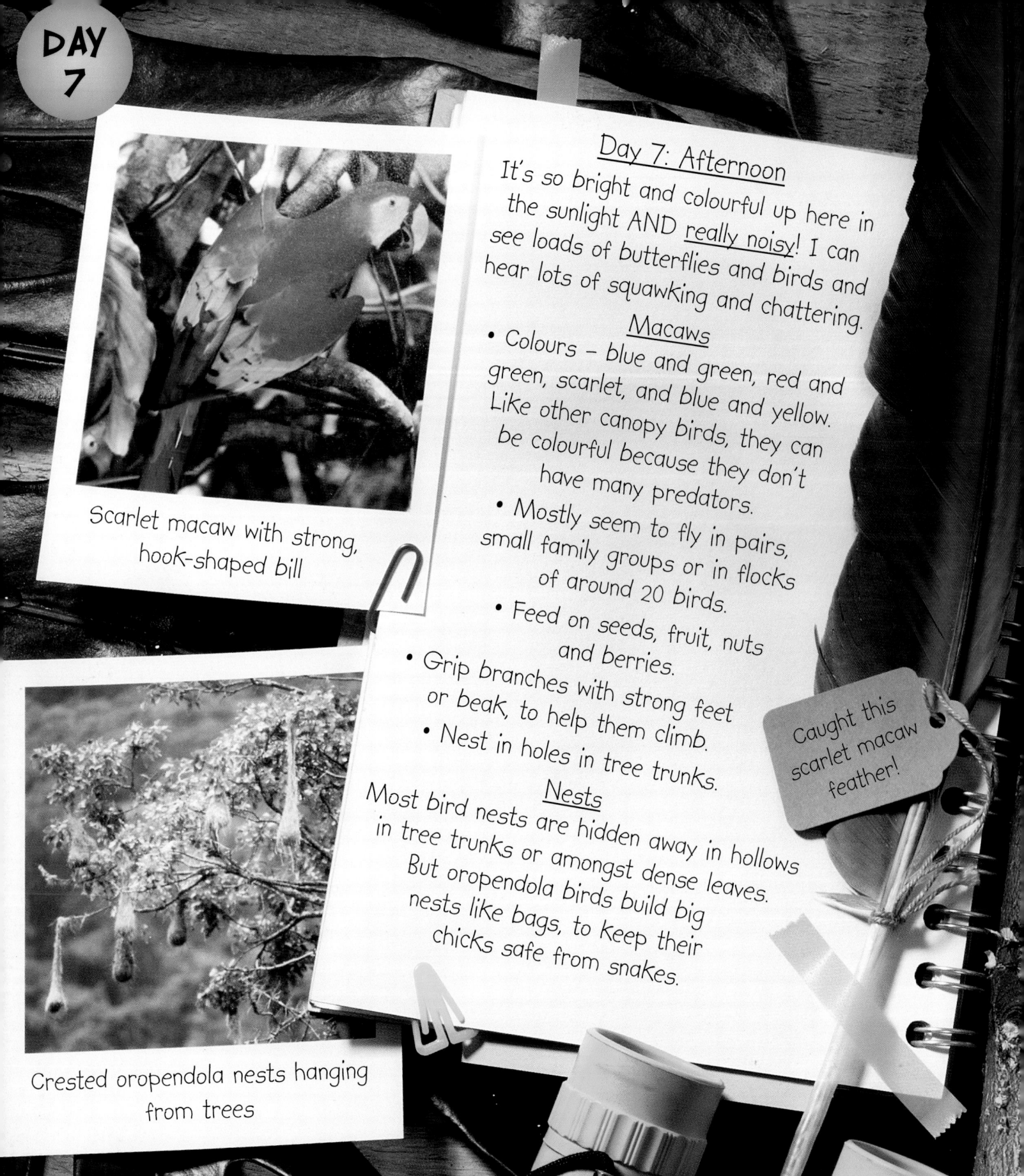

Scarlet macaw with strong,
hook-shaped bill

Crested oropendola nests hanging
from trees

Day 7: Afternoon

It's so bright and colourful up here in the sunlight AND <u>really noisy</u>! I can see loads of butterflies and birds and hear lots of squawking and chattering.

Macaws

- Colours – blue and green, red and green, scarlet, and blue and yellow. Like other canopy birds, they can be colourful because they don't have many predators.
- Mostly seem to fly in pairs, small family groups or in flocks of around 20 birds.
- Feed on seeds, fruit, nuts and berries.
- Grip branches with strong feet or beak, to help them climb.
- Nest in holes in tree trunks.

Nests

Most bird nests are hidden away in hollows in tree trunks or amongst dense leaves. But oropendola birds build big nests like bags, to keep their chicks safe from snakes.

Caught this scarlet macaw feather!

Beaks and bills

Birds' beaks are adapted to eat certain types of food. Macaws have strong, hooked beaks to help them crack open seeds and nuts, and to help them climb. Toucans have huge bills, sometimes bigger than the bird's body. It is not really known why their bills are so big, but they are useful for pecking out soft, juicy fruit or sucking up water. Toucan bills are light in weight because their internal bony structure is honeycombed rather than solid. But these big bills are too clumsy for building nests, so toucans generally nest in holes made by other birds.

Toucan bills are brightly coloured to warn off predators or help them find a mate.

The serrated edge of a toucan's large bill helps it grip its food.

Emergent tree facts

- The tops of emergent trees can grow up to 60 m tall, forming the highest layer in the rainforest.
- Emergent trees are widely spaced so their tops don't merge and form a continuous layer.
- Up to 80 species of different plants may live on a single emergent tree.
- Around 20% of rainforest birds live and nest in emergent trees, including the harpy eagle.
- The leaves of most emergent trees are usually thicker and more leathery than canopy leaves so they don't lose nutrients when water evaporates from them.

Special relationships

The rainforests are so lush and rich with such a variety of plant and animal life that many plants and animals have become highly specialised to avoid competition. Around 160 species of hummingbird live in the rainforest. They feed mainly on nectar, and most have long beaks, specially adapted to drink the nectar from particular flowers. The Brazil nut tree has a special relationship with a few types of bee. The tree has a kind of springy hood coiling over its stamens where nectar is produced. Only certain bees can lift up the hood to reach the sweet nectar inside.

The male crimson topaz hummingbird has brightly coloured plumage. It feeds on nectar from a wide range of rainforest flowers.

Have just read that a hummingbird's wings beat about 55 times a SECOND as it hovers!

Monkey business

(notes on how a black spider monkey swings through trees)

- Long limbs for swinging on branches.
- Long fingers and toes to grip branches.
- Very acrobatic – can cover 9–10 m in just one leap!
- Uses tail – for balance, to slow down when leaping and to hold onto branches.
- Part of the tail, near tip, is naked and patterned with grooves to help it grip.

Saw one spider monkey dangling from a branch by just its tail – it did look a bit like a spider!

Remember to keep looking for the world's largest eagle – the harpy eagle

Predators

Monkeys don't have many predators. One of the main ones is the harpy eagle (pictured), which swoops after its prey through the trees, plucking it off a branch with its huge talons, then carrying it back to its treetop nest. Other predators include pythons and the black hawk-eagle (also called the monkey-hawk by native Amazonians).

Saving the tamarin

Environmental report

The golden lion tamarin was once thought to be the most endangered primate in the world. In the 1970s, there were probably only 100 wild tamarins left, due mainly to the destruction of their forest habitat. Conservation programs started in the early 1970s have included setting up the Poco das Antas Biological Reserve in Brazil and starting captive breeding programs in zoos worldwide. These measures have been largely successful and the tamarins now have a greater chance of survival. There is now a stable population of over 480 tamarins in zoos and around 600 in the wild.

Some tamarins have been successfully reintroduced into their native habitat.

Red howler monkey

Range: Columbia to Bolivia, north and west Amazonia

Size: 80–90 cm body; 80–90 cm tail

Features: One of the largest New World monkeys. Feeds mainly on leaves and fruit. Males lead a troop of around 6 to 8 animals, and make loud calls to defend their territory from rival groups. Calls can be heard around 3 km away.

New World monkeys

There are two families of New World (American) monkeys

- marmosets and tamarins (about 20 species): tree-dwellers, but do not have grasping hands. Can't grip with tail (it is not <u>prehensile</u>).
- cebids, or flat-nosed monkeys (about 30–35 species, including capuchins, howler monkeys, woolly monkeys, spider monkeys, sakis and uakaris). Most have prehensile tails.

Monkey food

Mostly a mixture of fruit and leaves. Some monkeys also eat flowers, lizards, butterflies, baby birds, eggs or spiders.

↑ Yuk!

Monkey families

Most monkeys live in family groups or larger troops of 20 to 50 animals. They talk to each other with calls and cries.

Different species have either one or two babies. Most babies stay with their mother and drink her milk for several months or even up to two years.

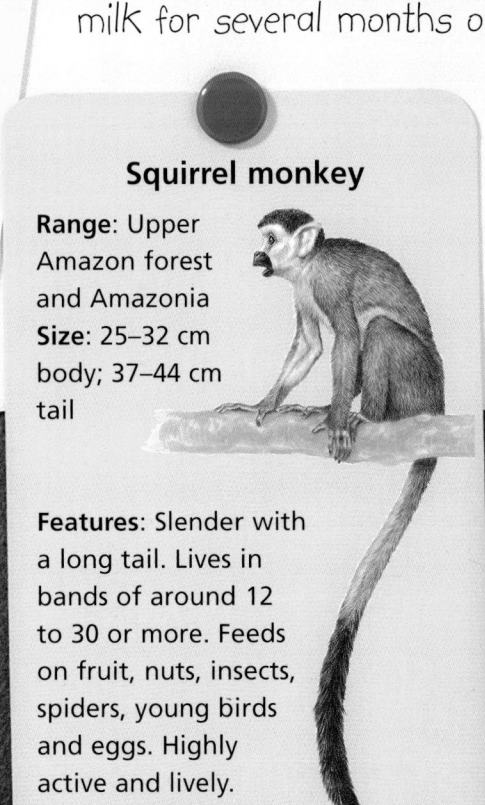

Squirrel monkey feeding on a flower!

Pygmy marmoset

Range: Western Amazonia and upper Amazon forest
Size: 11–15 cm body; 17–23 cm tail

Features: Small and light (like other marmosets and tamarins). Lives in trees but doesn't have grasping hands; instead it leaps straight from one tree-trunk to the next. Eats mainly fruit, insects, small birds and eggs. Lives in troops of 5 to 10 animals.

↑

The pygmy marmoset is the smallest monkey – small enough to sit in a breakfast bowl!

Squirrel monkey

Range: Upper Amazon forest and Amazonia
Size: 25–32 cm body; 37–44 cm tail

Features: Slender with a long tail. Lives in bands of around 12 to 30 or more. Feeds on fruit, nuts, insects, spiders, young birds and eggs. Highly active and lively.

White-fronted capuchin

Range: Upper Amazon Basin and western Amazonia
Size: 30–38 cm body; 38–50 cm tail
Features: Slender with long limbs and tail. Feeds on shoots, fruit, insects, young birds and eggs. Lives in groups of 20 or 30 animals.

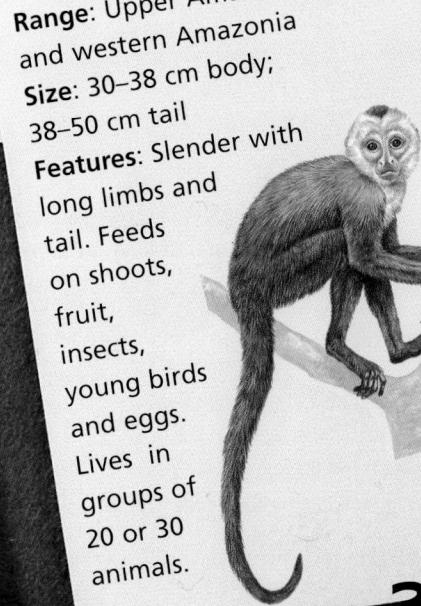

27

(Nearly) day 9

We are spending the whole night out in the rainforest! It's much noisier than I thought it would be. There is lots of rustling and creaking as nocturnal animals scurry about and forage for food. Managed to get this photo of a kinkajou, which had been feeding.

Saw some pale, whitish flowers that open only at night. They're pale to attract night-flying moths and bats that feed on their nectar.

Kinkajou hanging upside-down by its tail

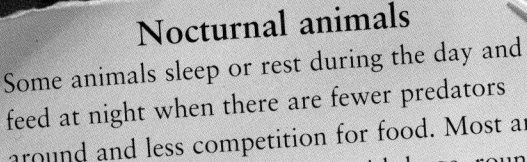

Hylocereus undatus

Nocturnal animals

Some animals sleep or rest during the day and feed at night when there are fewer predators around and less competition for food. Most are adapted for night-time vision with large, round eyes to collect as much light as possible and help them see in the dark. Common nocturnal mammals of the Amazon include the northern tamandua, a tree-dwelling anteater, the silky anteater and the tree porcupine. All have prehensile tails, which help them climb trees.

Tree porcupine

Night-time predators

One of the most common nocturnal predators is the owl. The great horned owl and the spectacled owl, both native to the Amazon rainforest, have such good vision that they can spot a small mammal, reptile, amphibian or a large insect moving through the branches from high in the treetops. They also have excellent hearing. Another night-time predator is the bushmaster snake. It hides during the day in a tree hollow, emerging at night to hunt small rodents and other mammals which it kills with a poisonous bite.

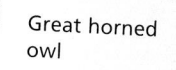

Great horned owl

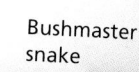

Bushmaster snake

Have just seen a Douroucouli (also called a night monkey or owl monkey)! It had big, round eyes with patches of white fur above them. Heard it squeak and make a kind of barking sound, but then it quickly scampered off...

It's the <u>only</u> true nocturnal monkey in the world. As well as fruit, it eats leaves, insects, spiders, small mammals, birds and bats. The white patches above its eyes are used as signalling devices (to communicate with its mate). During the day, it sleeps in small family groups wedged in the hollow of trees or hidden amongst the leaves.

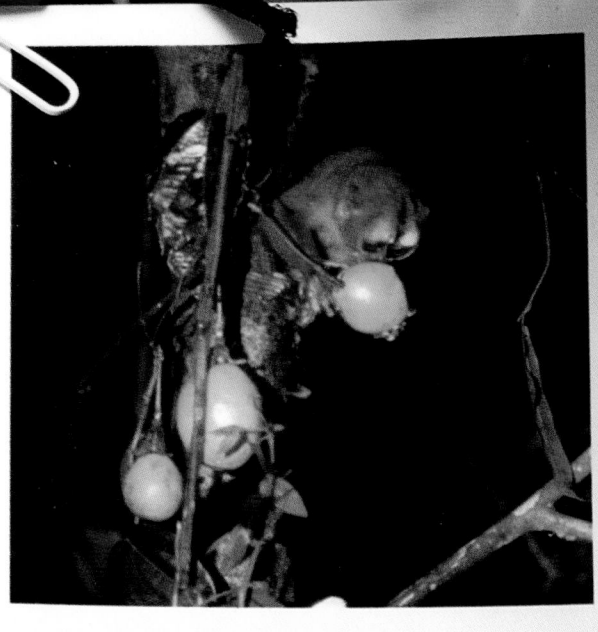

Douroucouli feeding on passiflora fruit

Spear-nosed, long-tongued bat feeding on banana flowers

Notes on bats

- Some feed on plants and fruits or drink nectar from flowers. Others catch and eat night-flying insects.
- Have poor eyesight but large ears and good hearing.
- Find their way around by echo-location – a kind of radar. The bats make sounds (usually ultrasonic) which bounce off objects all around and produce patterns that the bats recognise.
- Tropical bats don't hibernate like the bats of North America or Europe because they can find plenty of food all year round.

Spear-nosed bats drink nectar but prefer mice, birds and even smaller bats!

41

Day 11: Going home

Finally heading back downriver to Manaus. Felt really sad to be leaving the camp and miserable that I hadn't spotted a harpy eagle — made worse because a scientist we met gave me a photograph of a young harpy eagle that HE'D spotted a few kilometres from our camp. Then, this morning, an incredible thing happened — we actually saw an adult harpy eagle!!! It suddenly swooped right down from the trees and across the river, so close I could feel the air rush across my face from its beating wings. I didn't manage to get my camera out in time, but ← here's my sketch.

Out-stretched wings around 2 m wide →

Young harpy eagle in nest (NOT MY PHOTO!)

Ecotourism

A child learns to play a pipe from an Amazonian chief.

Environmental report

Ecotourism – visiting a natural environment to learn about its culture, animals and plants, rather than just sightseeing – is being promoted by many governments in rainforest countries. Although the tourists' money can be used for conservation and reforestation, if too many tourists visit an area its delicate ecosystem may be harmed or even destroyed.

Conserving the rainforests

Saving the rainforests is a huge and difficult problem. People all over the world must be educated about the importance of the rainforests and the precious resources they contain. Many organisations and governments are working to preserve the forests by setting up reserves where land cannot be developed or destroyed, and areas for controlled replanting.

Planting mahogany seedlings on a plantation in Brazil to provide timber resources. Other plants, such as Brazil nuts and cashews, are being grown and harvested over extended periods of time so that the rainforest ecosystem is not harmed.

Things to do back home

- Join a conservation group to help save the rainforests! • Adopt an endangered rainforest animal at my local zoo. • Do more recycling! • Stop eating beefburgers if the beef has been raised on cleared rainforest land.

Have just read that 40 hectares of tropical rainforest are destroyed every minute. So whilst I have been writing this, 20 hectares of rainforest have been lost!

Rainforest medicine

Medical report

Some scientists believe that as yet undiscovered rainforest plants may hold the cure for cancer. Around half of all medicines used today have their origins in plants from rainforests. Quinine, for example, is used to treat malaria, cortisone for arthritis, reserpine for anxiety and curare for tetanus. As the rainforests are cleared, thousands of species of plants that could be used to treat and cure people suffering from life-threatening illnesses, could be lost forever.

*Check out Rainforest Action Network web site (www.ran.org)

GLOSSARY

adaptation Process taking place usually over hundreds or thousands of years by which animals develop features or behaviour that helps them survive in a particular environment.

algae (singular: alga) Simple plants made of one or several cells with no true stems, roots or leaves. Most algae grow in fresh water and the sea although some live in damp soil and on tree trunks.

Amazonia The surrounding area that drains into the Amazon river. It is covered in lowland rainforest and waterways.

Amazonas A state in northwest Brazil, South America, consisting of the central Amazon basin and its vast areas of unexplored tropical rainforest. Its capital city is Manaus.

aquatic Living in water.

atmosphere The blanket of gases surrounding the Earth or another planet.

basin A large depression (sunken area) in the Earth's crust. It is also an area drained by rivers and tributaries.

billion One thousand million.

biodiversity (short for biological diversity) The wide variety of plant and animal life.

buttress root Support growing from the sides of a tree's trunk to support its weight.

camouflage Colours or markings on an animal's body to help it blend in with its surroundings to avoid predators, or to lie in wait for its prey.

carbon dioxide A gas with no smell or colour given out by animals and absorbed by plants. Too much carbon dioxide gas in the atmosphere results in global warming.

chlorofluorocarbons (CFCs) Gases made up from chlorine, fluorine and carbon which can damage the ozone layer.

climate The usual or average weather conditions in a particular area over a long period of time.

colony Large group of animals, such as ants, termites and some types of wasp and bee, that live together, usually in a nest.

conservation Protecting, preserving and managing the Earth's natural resources and the environment.

deciduous Tree that sheds all its leaves once a year at the end of its growing season.

decomposer Organism that breaks down dead and decaying material, such as animals and plants.

diversity (species) The variety of plants and animals that live in a particular area.

ecosystem A community of living things and their environment. Also called a biome.

epiphyte A plant, such as an orchid, bromeliad or fern that grows on another plant for support, absorbing nutrients from the air and rainwater. It doesn't harm the host plant. Some epiphytes live on high branches in strong sunlight; others live lower down in the damp and shade.

equator Imaginary line around the Earth's middle, separating the globe into two halves – the northern and southern hemispheres.

evaporation The process by which a liquid or solid is changed into a gas or vapour when it is heated.

extinct No longer exists anywhere in the world; many types of animal are in danger of extinction.

global warming The warming of the atmosphere due to pollution.

greenhouse effect A warming of the Earth's lower atmosphere, caused by the release of carbon dioxide gas from pollution such as smoke from factories and car exhaust fumes, which trap heat near the Earth's surface that would normally escape.

habitat The place or environment where a plant or animal lives.

hemisphere One half of a sphere. The Earth is divided by the equator into the northern hemisphere and the southern hemisphere.

humidity Amount of moisture in the air.

humus Decomposed organic matter.

indigenous Originating, or coming, from a particular place.

liana Type of climbing vine with a strong, woody stem that can grow around 900 m long. Lianas are used to make rattan furniture and baskets, and sometimes bridges across streams and small rivers.

litter Dead leaves, twigs and branches that fall and build up on a forest floor.

mimicry Copying the behaviour or features of another, more dangerous, animal to escape predators; for example, several species of butterfly and moth have large eyespots on their wings which look like the staring eyes of a bird.

nocturnal Active during the night rather than during the day.

nutrient Food needed by plants and animals to live and grow.

ozone layer Layer in the atmosphere where the gas ozone is concentrated.

parasitic Feeds on or inside another living creature, called a host.

photosynthesis Way in which green plants make sugary food from sunlight and carbon dioxide gas from the air. As they make food, they release oxygen and water into the air.

pollination When pollen is transferred from the male parts of a flower to the female parts of a flower and it begins to make seeds. Some plants pollinate themselves. Most, however, rely on the wind or animals such as insects, birds and bats, to spread their pollen.

prehensile A part of the body that is flexible and is able to grip or hold. For example, some monkeys have prehensile tails that they can use like another hand, to hold on to branches.

pupa Stage in the lifecycle of some insects, such as butterflies and moths, when they change from larvae to adults.

reserve Area set aside to protect wild plants and animals, particularly rare ones that are in danger of extinction.

slash and burn When land is cleared by slashing trees and bushes then burning them to release nutrients into the soil. The cleared land is used for farming or raising cattle.

soil The thin top layer of the land surface in which plants and trees grow. It is made up of a mixture of minerals, humus (organic matter), air and water.

strangler fig Plant that starts life as an epiphyte when its seeds are dropped by a brid or bat onto a treetop branch. Long roots grow down to the ground, eventually covering the tree until the tree rots away and dies.

subtropical Describes the landscape, climate and regions bordering the tropics.

temperate Typical climate conditions in the regions between the tropics and the polar regions. The temperatures in temperate regions are moderate, being neither very hot nor very cold.

transpiration The release of water into the air from green-leaved plants during photosynthesis.

tributary A smaller stream or river that runs into another, larger, stream or river.

tropical To do with the tropics – the hot, wet regions lying on or near the equator between the Tropic of Cancer and the Tropic of Capricorn.

Tropic of Cancer/Tropic of Capricorn Imaginary lines drawn around each of the Earth's hemispheres. The Tropic of Cancer is on the line of latitude that lies 23.5°N of the equator, in the northern hemisphere, and the Tropic of Capricorn is on the line of latitude that lies 23.5°S of the equator, in the southern hemisphere. The area (that surrounds the equator) between these two lines is the only area on Earth in which the Sun can be directly overhead.

venom A poisonous liquid used by an animal to kill or paralyse prey.

water vapour Water in the form of an invisible gas.

RAINFOREST CONSERVATION CHALLENGES

• Don't buy any products made out of tropical rainforest wood, such as rosewood, mahogany, teak and ebony.

• Use less paper and recycle any paper that you do use. Since most paper comes from trees, using less can help save the rainforests. Use 100% recycled paper whenever possible or tree-free paper made from plants, such as kenaf. You can also save paper by writing or drawing on both sides of one sheet and using towels and napkins made of cloth instead of paper.

• Don't eat beef if it's been raised on land that used to be rainforest land. Ask where the beef comes from. The Rainforest Action Network (RAN) estimates that 5 sq m of rainforest is destroyed to make every quarter-pound fast-food hamburger from beef raised on rainforest land.

• Look out for and buy products obtained from sustainable rainforest crops (when crops are harvested from a forest over long periods of time without damaging its ecosystem) to help support sustainable farming.

• Join a rainforest conservation group. For example, become a member of RAN's Kid's Action Team. See their web site (listed below) for details.

THINGS TO DO

• VISIT A BOTANICAL GARDEN
Many botanical gardens have a hothouse that recreates the atmosphere of a tropical rainforest so you can experience its heat and humidity and see the lushness and variety of its plant-life.

• VISIT A BUTTERFLY GARDEN
Large butterfly gardens often have a tropical hothouse where you can see colourful rainforest species flitting through the trees.

• VISIT YOUR LOCAL ZOO
See some rainforest animals close up and find out what the zoo is doing to help conserve endangered species. Some zoos have a scheme where you can adopt an animal for a fee (see below).

• VISIT AN AQUARIUM
Meet some of the fish that come from the Amazon Basin.

• PLANT A TREE
Plant a tree in your back garden or join an organisation involved in reforestation so you can help to add to the world's supply of oxygen.

• ADOPT AN ENDANGERED ANIMAL
For a fee, you can help save an individual animal and other animals of the same species through the WorldWide Fund for Nature (see their address below).

USEFUL ADDRESSES

Natural History Museum,
Cromwell Road,
London SW7 5BD
United Kingdom
Tel: 020 7942 5011
Web site: www.nhm.ac.uk

Friends of the Earth (UK)
26/28 Underwood Street
London N1 7JZ
United Kingdom
Tel: 020 7490 1555
Web site: foe.co.uk/

Friends of the Earth (Australia)
17 Lord Street
Newtown 2042
Australia
Tel: (02) 9517 3900
Web site: http:/www.foe.org.au/

Friends of the Earth International
(FoEI)
PO Box 19199
1000 G-D Amsterdam
The Netherlands
Tel: +31 20 6221369
Web site: http://www.foei.org/

World Wide Fund for Nature (UK)
Panda House
Weyside Park
Godalming
Surrey GU7 1XR
United Kingdom
Tel: 01483 426444
Web site: www.wwf-uk.org

Royal Society for Nature Conservation
(RSNC)
The Kiln, Waterside
Mather Road
Newark
Notts NG24 1WT
United Kingdom
Tel: 01636 670 000
Web site: www.rsnc.org

WEB SITES

www.ran.org
Rainforest Action Network (RAN) web site, with general rainforest information, action alerts, descriptions of current campaigns, kids' corner and information about joining RAN.

http://mbgnet.mobot.org
Homepage of the Evergreen Project Inc with information on types of forest and links to other organisations and projects related to the Amazon.

www.earth2kids.org
Test your rainforest knowledge and find out about rainforests around the world.

www.rainforest-alliance.org
Find out about conservation events and where to buy ecofriendly forest products; site includes a section for kids.

www.5tiger.org
Homepage of the Tiger Information Centre containing information and news on saving the remaining five sub-species of tiger around the world.

http://forests.org/forsite.html
Rainforest site which lists contacts to many other rainforest organisations.

INDEX

ACKNOWLEDGEMENTS

PICTURE CREDITS

Photography by Dave King

Photomontages by Ella Butler

Maps by Alan Collinson Design except front endpaper map which was done by Peter Bull Art Studio

Other art by: Graham Allen; Norman Arlott; Bob Bampton (Bernard Thornton Artists); Keith Brewer; Jim Channell (Bernard Thornton Artists); Joanne Cowne; Malcolm Ellis (Bernard Thornton Artists); Bridget James (Wildlife Art); Alan Male (Linden Artists); Colin Newman (Bernard Thornton Artists); Dick Twinney; Ken Wood; Michael Woods

PHOTOGRAPHIC CREDITS

l=left; r=right; b=bottom; t=top; c=centre; OSF = Oxford Scientific Films; BCC = Bruce Coleman Collection
All photography by Dave King except:
2 Michael Dick/Animals Animals/OSF; 3 Mark Edwards/Still Pictures; 6-7 Martin Wendler/Natural History Photographic Agency; 8t & b Staffan Widstrand/BCC; 9tl Staffan Widstrand/BCC; 9ct C.B. & D.W. Frith/BCC; 9cb Gerald S. Cubitt/BCC; 9 tr Mike Hill/OSF; 11t Nick Gordon/OSF; 11b Richard Packwood/OSF; 12-13 (Photomontage) Dr. F. Koster/OSF, Nick Gordon/OSF, David Macdonald/OSF, Michael Goulding/Partridge Films Ltd./OSF, Max Gibbs/OSF, Fabio Colombini/Animals Animals/OSF, Uwe Walz/BCC, David Cayless/OSF, Tony Allen/Green Films/OSF, Hans Reinhard/BCC, Max Gibbs/OSF; 14t Gunter Ziesler/BCC; 14b Nick Gordon/OSF; 15b Tony Morrison/South American Pictures; 16t David Cayless/OSF; 16b Max Gibbs/OSF; 17tl Ken Cole/Animals Animals/OSF; 17tc Gunter Ziesler/BCC; 17tr Dr. F. Koster/Survival Anglia/OSF; 18-19 (Photomontage) Michael Fogden/BCC, Dr. F. Koster/Survival Anglia/OSF; André Bärtschi/Planet Earth Pictures, David Lazenby/Planet Earth Pictures, Geoff Kidd/OSF, Staffan Widstrand/BCC, Paul Franklin/OSF, Carl Wallace/BCC; 20t André Bärtschi/Planet Earth Pictures; 20c David Fox/OSF; 20b John Cancalosi/BCC; 21b Carl Wallace/BCC; 22t Michael Fogden/BCC; 22cAlastair Shay/OSF; 22b Michael Fogden/OSF; 23t Paul Franklin/OSF; 24–25 (Photomontage) P.K. Sharpe/OSF, Patti Murray/ Animals Animals/OSF, Michael Fogden/BCC, Eric Soder/Natural History Photographic Agency, Staffan Widstrand/BCC, Jim Clare/Partridge Films Ltd./OSF, Zig Leszczynski/Animals Animals/OSF, Michael Fogden/OSF; 26b Jany Sauvanet/Natural History Photographic Agency; 27t Brian Rogers/Natural Visions; 28t Michael Fogden/BCC; 29tl Zig Leszczynski/Animals Animals/OSF; 29tr G.I. Bernard/OSF; 29b Michael Fogden/OSF; 30–31 (Photomontage) Luiz Claudio Marigo/BCC, Michael Fogden/OSF, Staffan Widstrand/BCC, Luiz Claudio Marigo/BCC, Breck P. Kent/Animals Animals/OSF, Dr. Eckhart Pott/BCC, Tom Ulrich/OSF, Staffan Widstrand/BCC, Manfred Pfefferle/OSF; 32 Konrad Wothe/BCC; 33 Heather Angel/Natural Visions; 34t BCC; 34b Jurgen & Christine Sohns/Frank Lane Picture Agency; 36 Michael Sewell/OSF; 37 BCC; 38-39 (Photomontage) Aldo Brando/OSF, Stephen Dalton/OSF, Partridge Films Ltd./OSF, P.J. DeVries/OSF, 39 Michael Fogden/OSF, Haroldo Palo Jr./Natural History Photographic Agency; Rod Williams/BCC, Jim Clare/Partridge Films Ltd./OSF; 40 Aldo Brando/OSF; 41t Nick Gordon/OSF; 41b Gunter Ziesler/BCC; 42 Tui de Roy/OSF; 43t Michael Doolittle/Still Pictures; 43b Mark Edwards/Still Pictures
Cover photography by Dave King except for the following: Anaconda: Nick Gordon/OSF; Squirrel monkey: Bruce Coleman Collection

A Marshall Edition
Edited and designed by
Marshall Editions Ltd
The Orangery
161 New Bond Street
London W1S 2UF
www.marshallpublishing.com

Original concept by Sue Nicholson

First published in the UK in 2001 by Marshall Publishing Ltd

Copyright © 2001 Marshall Editions Developments Ltd

Originated in Italy by Articolor
Printed and bound in Italy by Officine Grafiche de Agostini
10 9 8 7 6 5 4 3 2 1

ISBN 1 84028 482 X

Consultant:	Dr Helen Newing
Editor:	Claire Sipi
Designer:	Siân Williams
Jacket Designer:	Steve Woosnam-Savage
Editorial Manager:	Kate Phelps
Art Director:	Simon Webb
Publishing Director:	Linda Cole
Proofreader:	Jane Chapman
Indexer:	Jean Clarke
Production:	Christina Schuster
Picture Researcher:	Frances Vargo
Research:	Julia March

RAINFOREST SPOTTER'S GUIDE

Can you spot these rainforest dwellers
in the photographic scenes in the book?

Common squirrel monkey (body 25–32 cm)

Common iguana (size 1–2 m)

Nine-banded armadillo (body 35–58 cm)

Emerald hummingbird (size 8 cm)

White-faced capuchin (body 33–45 cm)

Hoatzin (size 61 cm)

Kinkajou (body 39–54 cm)

Zebra butterfly (wingspan 7.5–8 cm)

Red piranha (size up to 30.5 cm)

Spectacled owl (size 43–46 cm)

Tambaqui fish (size up to 1 m)

Jaguar (body 1.1–1.8 m)

Three-toed sloth (body 46–75 cm)

Tamandua (body 53–88 cm)

Scarlet macaw (size 84 cm)

Bushmaster (size 2.45–3.5 m)

Great vampire bat (body 7.5–9 cm)

Blue and yellow macaw (size 84 cm)

Hercules beetle (size up to 18 cm)

Emerald tree boa (size 1.2 m)

Coati (body 47–58 cm)

Tree porcupine (body 44–56 cm)